WORLD ALMANAC® LIBRARY OF
★ THE CIVIL WAR ★

The Civil War at Sea

Dale Anderson

WORLD ALMANAC® LIBRARY

Please visit our web site at: www.worldalmanaclibrary.com
For a free color catalog describing World Almanac® Library's
list of high-quality books and multimedia programs,
call 1-800-848-2928 (USA) or 1-800-387-3178 (Canada).
World Almanac® Library's fax: (414) 332-3567.

Library of Congress Cataloging-in-Publication Data

Anderson, Dale, 1953-
   The Civil War at sea / by Dale Anderson.
      p. cm. — (World Almanac Library of the Civil War)
   Includes bibliographical references and index.
   ISBN 0-8368-5585-X (lib. bdg.)
   ISBN 0-8368-5594-9 (softcover)
   1. United States—History—Civil War, 1861-1865—Naval
operations—Juvenile literature. [1. United States—History—
Civil War, 1861-1865—Naval operations.] I. Title. II. Series.
E591.A55   2004
973.7'5—dc22   2003062490

First published in 2004 by
World Almanac® Library
330 West Olive Street, Suite 100
Milwaukee, WI 53212 USA

Copyright © 2004 by World Almanac® Library.

Produced by Discovery Books
Project editor: Geoff Barker
Editor: Valerie J. Weber
Designer and page production: Laurie Shock, Shock Design, Inc.
Photo researcher: Rachel Tisdale
Consultant: Andrew Frank, Assistant Professor of History, Florida
      Atlantic University
Maps: Stefan Chabluk
World Almanac® editorial direction: Mark Sachner
World Almanac® art direction: Tammy Gruenewald

Photo credits: Peter Newark's American Pictures: cover, pp. 9
(bottom), 11, 16 (bottom), 25, 27 (bottom), 28, 30, 33, 37, 40, 41;
Corbis: pp. 6, 8, 24, 26, 27 (top), 32, 34, 35, 39 (left); Library of
Congress: title page, pp. 2, 7, 9 (top), 10, 12, 13, 16 (top), 18, 19, 20,
21, 23, 29, 36, 39 (right), 42.

Printed in the United States of America

1 2 3 4 5 6 7 8 9 08 07 06 05 04

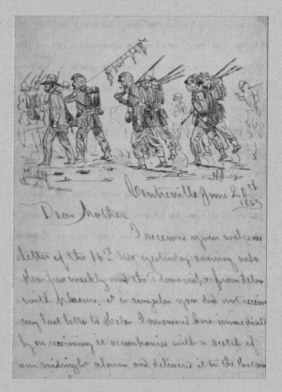

Cover: The Union ship *Hartford* (left) blasts away at the
Confederate ironclad *Manassas* during the Union move
to capture the key port of New Orleans. The use of
ironclads in the Civil War signaled a dramatic new era
for the world's navies.

*"To my mother, who got me
Bruce Catton; my brother,
who shared my passion for the
Civil War; and my wife and
sons, who cheerfully put up
with several field trips and
countless anecdotes."*

— DALE ANDERSON

Contents

Capital cities
Union States
Confederate States
Seceded from Virginia
Border States
United States Territories

Confederate and Union States in 1861

While the Confederate states covered about as much territory as the Union states, they held fewer people, fewer factories, and fewer railroad tracks and locomotives. These would be significant drawbacks for the Confederacy during the Civil War. The South would also lose part of its support when West Virginia separated from the rest of Virginia in 1863.

The War between the States

The Civil War was fought between 1861 and 1865. It was the bloodiest conflict in United States history, with more soldiers killed and wounded than in any other war. It was also a pivotal event in U.S. history: It transformed the lives of millions of African-American men, women, and children by freeing them from slavery.

It also transformed the nation, changing it from a loose confederation of states into a powerful country with a strong central government.

On one side were eleven southern states that had split from the United States to form a new country, the Confederate States of America, led by President Jefferson Davis. They took this step after Abraham Lincoln was elected president of the United

States in 1860. Southerners feared Lincoln would end slavery, which was central to their economy and society. The northern states, or the **Union**, declared this split illegal.

A big question was whether the four **Border States** (Delaware, Maryland, Kentucky, and Missouri) would join the **Confederacy**. They had slavery, too, but they also held many people loyal to the Union. To keep control of these states, Lincoln felt early in the war that he could not risk moving against slavery, fearing that to do so would drive the Border States out of the Union. Later, though, he did declare the emancipation, or freedom, of Southern slaves.

In the Border States, and in many others, families divided sharply, with some men fighting for one side and some for the other. The Civil War has been called a war of "brother against brother."

Fighting broke out on April 12, 1861, when gunners for the South began shelling Union soldiers in Fort Sumter in Charleston Harbor, South Carolina. This attack led Lincoln to call for troops to put down what he called an armed rebellion. Thousands of Northerners flocked to the Union army. Thousands of Southerners joined the Confederate army, deter-mined to win independence for their side.

Soldiers in both the Union and Confederate armies suffered the hard-ships—and occasional boredom—of life in an army camp. They also fought in huge battles with great bravery and heroism. At times, both sides treated their enemies with honor and respect. At other times, they treated them with cruelty and brutality.

The opposing armies fought in two main areas, or theaters. The east-ern theater included Pennsylvania, Virginia, and Maryland; the region near the Confederate capital of Richmond, Virginia; and the Union capital of Washington, D.C. The huge western theater stretched from east-ern Kentucky and Tennessee down to the Gulf of Mexico and all the way to New Mexico. By the end of the many bloody battles across these lands, the Union won in 1865, and the states reunited into a single country.

Most of the fighting in the Civil War took place on land, where huge armies clashed in bitter fighting that killed and wounded thousands of soldiers in each battle. Merchant ships and fighting ships also played an important role in the war efforts of both the Union and the Confederacy.

CHAPTER ONE

Men and Ships

~

Like a traditional ship, the U.S. Navy's *Pensacola* had sails, but as the
smokestack in the center reveals, this newer ship was also steam powered.

The U.S. Navy Before the War

When the Civil War began in 1861, the U.S. Navy was not ready for combat. It
was small, with three major problems.

First, many of its ships were old. The navy had started to modernize in the 1850s,
building several ships powered by steam as well as sails and outfitting many ships with
newer, more powerful guns. Still, about half the fleet was old sailing ships.

Second, many officers were also old. For decades, the navy lacked a policy forcing officers to retire, so they stayed in the service until late in life. As a result, younger officers had few hopes of rising in rank, and many left the service. Again, the navy had tried to fix this problem by creating a retirement policy, but many older officers remained when the war broke out.

Third, the navy was not prepared for the kind of war it would have to fight. Few ships could sail into the shallow harbors found in most of the South, and officers had little experience fighting on rivers or working with army units.

To meet these problems, President Abraham Lincoln chose Gideon Welles as secretary of the navy for the Union, or the North. An excellent choice, Welles was an able administrator with a good mind for strategy.

The Confederacy's Difficult Beginnings

The Confederacy, or the South, faced its own obstacles at the start of the Civil War. Its secretary of the navy, Stephen Mallory, had served on the U.S. Senate committee overseeing the navy in the 1850s. He, too, was an excellent secretary. One historian has judged that, considering the obstacles he faced, his job was "little short of phenomenal."

Those obstacles were substantial. First, the South had almost no navy. As

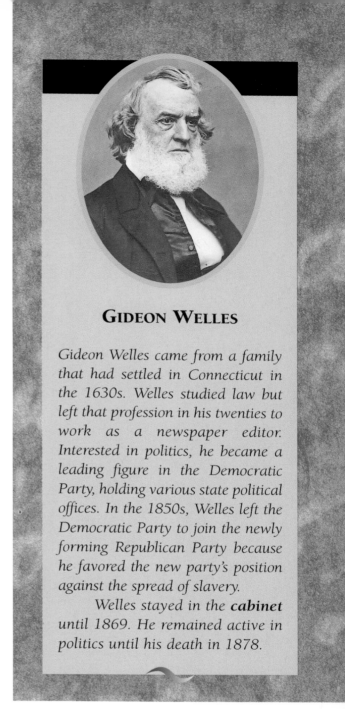

GIDEON WELLES

Gideon Welles came from a family that had settled in Connecticut in the 1630s. Welles studied law but left that profession in his twenties to work as a newspaper editor. Interested in politics, he became a leading figure in the Democratic Party, holding various state political offices. In the 1850s, Welles left the Democratic Party to join the newly forming Republican Party because he favored the new party's position against the spread of slavery.

Welles stayed in the **cabinet** *until 1869. He remained active in politics until his death in 1878.*

the Confederacy was being formed, Mallory could seize or buy only a handful of ships with a total of merely fifteen guns. Worse, the South contained only two large shipbuilding

yards. Worse yet, it lacked the industry required to build the engines or guns it would need for new ships. Finally, the South had little money to overcome all these other problems.

Nevertheless, Mallory worked miracles. He bought what ships he could, adding guns to them. He took control of all shipyards and set them to work building warships. He also built factories to make gunpowder, engines, and cannons. By the end of 1861, he had more than thirty ships afloat. As the years passed, he added more.

The North Updates Its Fleet

Despite its own naval problems, the Union did have several considerable advantages over the Confederacy. It contained many shipyards that could be hired to build warships. It also had money to buy already built ships and turn them into warships by adding guns. By the end of 1861, the Union had bought nearly eighty steamships and almost sixty sailing ships. These vessels were fitted with more than five hundred guns. Welles also launched an ambitious building program.

Officers and Men

In the land war, the North was badly hurt by the loss of many skilled generals who decided to fight for the South. That proved less

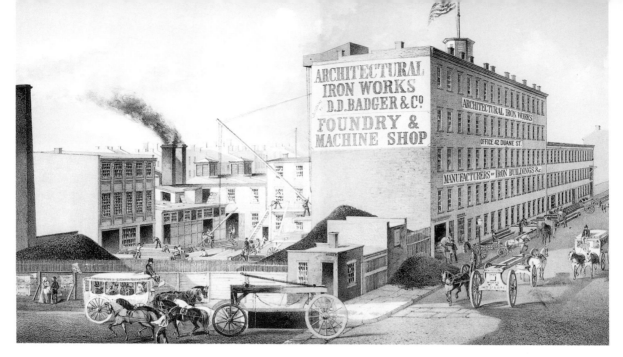

Iron works like this New York City plant gave the Union the ability to build the ships it needed.

of a problem for the navy, although several talented commanders did leave to join the Confederate navy. Raphael Semmes, for example, would plague Northern shipping for several years during the war, while James D. Bulloch bought many ships in Europe for the South's use. Nearly twelve hundred out of fifteen hundred naval officers stayed with the Union, however.

Ships held mammoth guns like these below the main deck. They rolled back from the gun port (an opening in the ship's side) on metal tracks so they could be reloaded.

In addition, the Union had another valuable resource for its navy. Northern, especially New England, businessmen owned most of the U.S. **merchant fleet.** Carrying trade goods, these ships operated from Northern ports. The captains and other officers on these ships were called upon to provide officers for the North's growing navy.

CHAPTER TWO

Early Action and Blockade

*"The power confided to me
will be used to hold, occupy, and possess
the property and places belonging to the government
. . . but beyond what may be necessary for these
objects, there will be no invasion, no using of force
against or among the people anywhere."*

President Abraham Lincoln in his first inaugural address, 1861

Harbor Forts

The first military crisis that both sides faced in the Civil War involved naval issues. When the Southern states **seceded** from the Union, they took possession of most facilities of the federal (now Union) government. However, two forts remained in Union hands—Fort Pickens in the harbor of Pensa-

Fort Pickens, off Pensacola, Florida, was easier for the Union to reinforce than Fort Sumter because it sat outside the range of Confederate guns on the shore.

cola, Florida, and Fort Sumter, in the harbor of Charleston, South Carolina. In his **inaugural** address, President Abraham Lincoln had vowed to hold all federal property in the South; that meant keeping the two forts.

Holding both, however, would prove difficult because both needed **reinforcements**. More importantly, the troops at Fort

This print dramatically shows the shelling of Fort Sumter that launched the Civil War. The small Union garrison there suffered thirty-three hours of shelling before surrendering.

Sumter needed more food or they could not hold out. Fort Pickens was reinforced, keeping it in federal hands.

Lincoln then skillfully put Confederate president Jefferson Davis in a box. He told Southern officials that he was sending an expedition to Fort Sumter with only food, clothes, and medicines for the Union soldiers. There would be no attempt to send weapons or land troops, he said, unless the fort was attacked first. The Confederates did not want the Sumter **garrison** to receive these supplies, since if the soldiers did, they could stay in the fort longer and use its guns to control shipping into and out of Charleston. The Confederates decided to open fire before the relief expedition reached the fort. The shelling of Fort Sumter on April 12, 1861, marked the beginning of the Civil War. The next day, the Union troops at Fort Sumter surrendered.

Competing Plans

When the war broke out, neither North nor South had a comprehensive plan for how to win it. Both, however, wanted to control the waterways.

Winfield Scott, top commander of the U.S. Army, developed the North's plan. He thought the navy should **blockade** Southern ports and work with the army to seize control of the Mississippi River. The blockade would prevent the Confederacy from getting badly needed supplies. Seizing the Mississippi would split the South, pre-venting states west of the river—Texas, Arkansas, and Louisiana—from sending supplies to states to the east. Holding the great river would also allow Union armies to move quickly up and down that waterway whenever they wanted.

Though it took a long time, Scott's plan worked. From 1861 to the middle of 1863, Union armies—aided by navy ships—seized several Confederate forts along the river. With the fall of both Vicksburg, Mississippi, and Port Hudson,

SEWARD OVERSTEPS HIS BOUNDS

The issue of relieving the two Union forts, Pickens and Sumter, led to an internal power struggle that threatened Lincoln's Cabinet. Secretary of State William Seward secretly issued orders to naval officers that went against commands issued by Secretary of the Navy Gideon Welles. Welles learned of Seward's directives accidentally and revoked them, reproaching the secretary of state for interfering in naval affairs. Lincoln sided with Welles and apologized for the fact that he had signed Seward's orders without consulting Welles. Seward also apologized and promised never to interfere with the navy again.

Early in the war, Secretary of State William Seward tried to take control of Lincoln's government, but the president stopped him. Thereafter, Seward served Lincoln well.

Louisiana, in July 1863, the Union gained control of the river.

The South's chief goal was to keep goods flowing into the South. It needed some ships to defend the ports and rivers and others to carry necessary supplies. To bring supplies, the South turned to **blockade-runners**, cargo vessels fast enough to outrun the ships enforcing the blockade. Their story is told in Chapter 3.

Confederate leaders also wanted to hurt the Union's merchant fleet, hoping to weaken the Union by cutting into its trade with other countries. This effort is described in Chapter 5.

Southern leaders thought they had an important weapon—cotton.

The textile mills of Britain and France used Southern cotton to make cloth. Southerners believed they could shut down those mills by not sending any cotton to Europe, which would force company owners to pressure European governments to recognize the South. Once it was seen as an independent nation, the South could get badly needed aid from those countries.

This "King Cotton" strategy backfired. The cotton crops of 1859 and 1860 had been large, and European mills had extra cotton on hand when the war began. Since mill owners did not suffer, they did not pressure their governments. Meanwhile, cotton rotted on Southern docks instead of being

Bales of cotton and other goods piled up on the docks of Southern ports, as Confederate leaders tried their "King Cotton" strategy.

sold to raise money the South badly needed. Eventually, the South began shipping cotton out on blockade-runners.

Presidential Actions

Soon after Fort Sumter, both presidents took action toward their goals of controlling the waterways. On April 17, 1861, President Davis offered **commissions** to privateers, privately owned ships that captured enemy merchant ships. Privateers received no payment from the government, earning money by selling the cargoes and

"Who will be hurt most [by the blockade]—us? themselves? or England? Not us, for we make the necessities of life—but what will England do for cotton—when her looms are idle?"

Southerner Catherine Deveraux Edmonston, in her diary, 1861

the ships they captured. Two days later, President Lincoln issued his own proclamation. First, he declared that captured privateers would be treated as criminals, as pirates. Second, he proclaimed a blockade of Southern ports.

Difficult Issues

The blockade raised a legal problem. In declaring it, Lincoln seemed to be recognizing the South as a foreign country since international law held that a country at war with another country could legally blockade that country. The move thus appeared to open the door to other countries recognizing the South—something Lincoln wanted to avoid just as desperately as the South wanted it to happen. Indeed, recognition went directly against Lincoln's statements that secession was illegal and that the war was a matter of putting down an internal rebellion.

The blockade also raised a practical problem. For other nations to recognize the blockade as legal, it had to be effective. The Union, however, did not have to block every single ship from entering or leaving Confederate ports; it only had to make running the

LEGAL DISPUTE

The crew of a privateer ship called the Savannah was indeed captured and tried for piracy. If convicted, they would have been hanged. Jefferson Davis's protests against this fate were ignored. Then Davis ordered an equal number of Union officers, held as prisoners of war, to be chosen for the same treatment. After that, the Union government backed down and dropped the piracy charges.

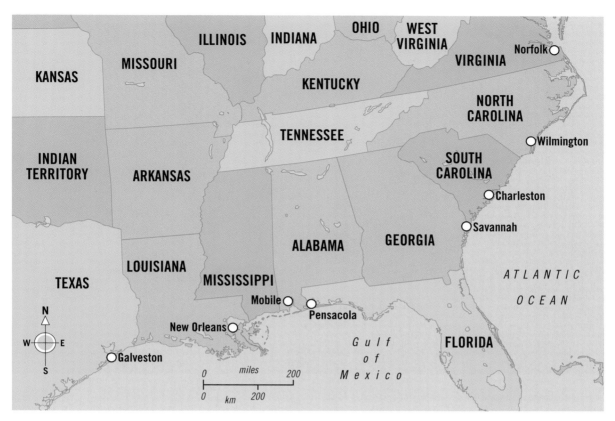

The South had four major ports on the Atlantic Ocean and four on the Gulf of Mexico. By preventing traffic into and out of these ports, the Union could make its blockade effective.

blockade dangerous. By the fall of 1861, British officials concluded that the blockade met that standard. As a result, it was legal in the eyes of other nations. Since these nations recognized the blockade, they could not officially trade with the Confederacy.

Producing an effective blockade was a daunting task. The Union navy simply did not have enough ships to block 3,500 miles (5,600 kilometers) of coast. However, much of that long coastline could not be used by large

ships. Knowing this, Lincoln had proclaimed a blockade only of the South's ports. The Union navy, then, only had to block trade from a few cities: Norfolk, Virginia; Wilmington, North Carolina; Charleston, South Carolina; Savannah, Georgia; Pensacola, Florida; Mobile, Alabama; New Orleans, Louisiana; and Galveston, Texas.

The Southeast

The North also moved to take control of smaller harbors in the South. In

Union ships blasted the two Confederate forts guarding Port Royal. One of those forts is visible beneath the Confederate flag on the left.

August 1861, the Union navy captured two forts that guarded the Hatteras Inlet in northeastern North Carolina, blocking the South's use of harbors there. Then the navy took Port Royal, south of Charleston, South Carolina.

Along with the loss of the harbors, these fights were ominous for the South in another way. For many long years, naval strategists had thought that forts could hold out against the guns on board ships. However, the more powerful guns on the newer Union ships were too strong and tore the forts to pieces.

John Dahlgren poses with one of the powerful naval guns he had designed before the war. A captain when the war broke out, Dahlgren rose to the rank of Union admiral.

Beating the Blockade

CHAPTER THREE

*"All these things, combined
with the delightful feeling of security
from capture, and the glorious prospect of a
good night's rest in [a real bed], wound one up
into an inexpressible state of jollity."*

Blockade-runner Charles Augustus Hobart-Hampden, remembering
what it was like to safely reach port, 1887

Creating the Blockade

The Union moved quickly to establish its blockade. By July of 1861, the Southern cities of Norfolk, Charleston, Pensacola, Mobile, New Orleans, and Wilmington were all blockaded. Savannah remained in Southern hands until late in the war. Galveston was captured by the Union and then retaken by the Confederates. Still, the blockade outside both ports remained effective.

Eventually, the Union blockade fleets were organized into four groups. The North Atlantic and South Atlantic squadrons divided the east coast. The East Gulf and West Gulf squadrons patrolled ports on the Gulf of Mexico.

Blockade-Runners

The Civil War was largely a land war, but control of trade over the seas was important for both sides. The Union's blockade shut down much trade to the South, but it did not end it completely. Many Confederate blockade-runners got through and helped the South survive.

This photograph, taken in 1865 off South Carolina's coast, shows the skeleton of a blockade-runner that had run aground on Sullivan's Island.

HIDING IN SMOKE

At least once, using very smoky coal worked to a blockade-runner's advantage. In 1863, a fast Union ship was chasing the Robert E. Lee, *commanded by John Wilkinson. After many hours, Wilkinson could still not shake his pursuers. He knew that his ship would be impossible to see when it turned dark. By burning soft coal and coal dust, he created huge billows of smoke. Then he stopped the smoke and quickly changed course, the shift hidden by the smoke and darkness. The pursuing ship followed his original course, while Wilkinson got away.*

The blockade-runners had special design features. They rode high in the water, even when fully loaded, so they would not get stuck on sandbars. They were built to be fast so they could outrun Union ships; they were safe early in the war if they could steam at 10 knots, or 10 nautical miles (11 miles [18 km]), an hour. As the Union built faster ships, blockade-runners needed more speed. Low masts made them less likely to be seen from far away, and most ships were painted gray so they blended into the sea at a distance. They steamed into port at night and never sailed under a full moon. Typically, captains of blockade-runners pre-

The *Robert E. Lee*, the famous blockade-runner owned by the Confederate government, is shown here after it was captured and renamed the USS *Fort Donelson*. Under that name, Union sailors used it to chase down other blockade-runners.

ferred burning coal that made as little smoke as possible.

The Confederate government itself owned a few of the blockade-runners. Private investors, however, including British business-people, owned the great majority of blockade-runners.

What They Carried

On the voyage from the South, the blockade-runners carried cotton bought in the South for 6 to 8 cents a

"From March 1, 1864, to January 1, 1865, the value of the shipments of cotton on Confederate government account was . . .$5,296,000 in [gold]."

Confederate government report, 1865

pound and sold in Britain for anywhere from 25 cents to $1 a pound, depending on the period of the war. These prices brought tremendous profits, which is what attracted investors to the dangerous trade. Ships owned by the Confederate government also sold cotton, which raised money for the government.

On the return trip, the privately owned ships generally brought back luxury goods like wine and silk that could be sold at a profit to wealthy

JOHN WILKINSON

John Wilkinson was born into a naval family from Virginia. In fact, his father was at sea on the USS Hornet *when John was born. Wilkinson followed his father into the navy in the 1840s and was commissioned as a lieutenant in 1850. In 1861, he joined the Confederate navy. He was captured when the Union took New Orleans and spent three months in prison in Boston, Massachusetts.*

After his release, Wilkinson commanded the Robert E. Lee, *running the blockade more than twenty times. After the war, Wilkinson lived for a while in Canada and then returned to his native Virginia. He eventually moved to Annapolis, Maryland, where he taught boys preparing for the U.S. Naval Academy.*

Southerners. The ships devoted most of their cargo space to these profit-making goods, but a small part of the cargo area was set aside to carry military goods needed by the government. Not until 1864, however, did the government strictly enforce the use of that space.

Still, the blockade-runners did bring a vast amount of valuable supplies. The Southern army that fought at Shiloh, Tennessee, in April 1862, for example, used guns and ammunition brought in by the *Fingal.* The Confederate government stated that the runners brought in more than 110,000 guns and huge amounts of powder and bullets between September 1862 and September 1863.

"[A Confederate official told me] Lee's army was in terrible straits, and had in fact rations only for about thirty days. . . . After some negotiations, he undertook to pay me a profit of 350 percent upon any provisions and meat I could bring in within the next three weeks."

Captain Thomas Taylor, recalling a deal to run the blockade, 1896

Prints were made to celebrate wartime victories, like this one showing the
capture of the *Armstrong, a* blockade-runner.

From December 1863 to December 1864, they carried about 500,000 pairs of shoes, 300,000 blankets, 8 million pounds (3.6 million kilograms) of meat, and 500,000 pounds (225,000 kg) of coffee. The South probably could not have lasted as long as it did without the blockade-runners.

One of the more unusual cargoes was carried by John Wilkinson on his first voyage commanding the *Robert E. Lee.* Along with guns and medical supplies, he brought twenty-six engravers from Scotland to engrave the plates from which the Confederacy would print paper money.

Cracking Down

As the war progressed, the blockade became more effective. The North was able to put more—and faster—ships into service, some of them former blockade-runners. A wily captain like Wilkinson could take advantage of this situation. He once escaped a fleet of Union ships by flying the United States flag, pretending that he, too, was patrolling to catch those running the blockade.

Union sailors had an incentive to capture blockade-runners; the government paid bonuses to ships that captured these vessels. By the end of the war, the government had paid out about $10 million in these bonuses. In all, the Union navy captured nearly 1,150 ships. More than 350 more were sunk or otherwise destroyed.

Despite the dangers, most runners were skillful enough to get through. By one estimate, more than three-quarters of the voyages ships made using ports in the Carolinas succeeded in running the blockade.

CHAPTER FOUR

Experiments in War

"I regard the possession of an iron-armored ship as a matter of the first necessity. . . . Naval success dictate[s] the wisdom and expediency of fighting with iron against wood."

Stephen Mallory, message to the
Confederate Congress, 1862

Making Gunboats

Early in the war, fighting in the West focused on control of the rivers, especially the Mississippi. Both sides wanted command of the rivers so they could control shipping of troops and supplies. To take rivers from the Confederates, the Union needed a combination of army and navy power. James Eads, a St. Louis engineer, signed a contract to build seven gunboats to help in this effort. The brilliant Eads worked his shipbuilding crews around the clock seven days a week. Holding thirteen guns, the boats were long, low vessels, good for moving along the shallow rivers. Most importantly, they were ironclads, or ships with iron plating covering the raised structure to strengthen it. Covering ships with metal was a new tactic in the Civil War.

Eads's gunboats helped Union forces capture Fort Henry and Fort Donelson on the Tennessee and Cumberland Rivers in February 1862. They also figured in the capture of Island No. 10 in Missouri two months later, which gave the North control over the upper Mississippi River.

Building the *Virginia*

The South had its own new ships. Early in the war, a Confederate force captured a U.S. Navy ship called the *Merrimac* by taking the Norfolk navy yard where it was docked. Union soldiers had tried to destroy all the ships there, but *Merrimac's* hull and engine had gone undamaged. Confederate secretary Mallory thought that ironclad ships armed with **rams** were his best weapons against Union ships blocking Southern ports. He ordered the ship turned into an ironclad.

The Confederates topped the ship with a sloping structure—with ten cannons inside—covered with two layers of iron plates. They also put an iron ram in front. Now named the *Virginia*, the new ship was a formidable vessel, as it quickly proved.

On March 8, 1862, the *Virginia* steamed toward the Union blockading fleet off Norfolk. It quickly rammed the *Cumberland*, sinking it. The *Congress*, trying to flee, ran aground,

JAMES B. EADS

James B. Eads was born in Indiana, but his family moved often, as his father had little success in business. Because of the moves, Eads had little formal education.

*Eventually, the family ended up in St. Louis, Missouri. At eighteen, Eads began serving on a Mississippi riverboat, which led him to think about making money by recovering goods lost when boats sank. He invented a **diving bell** that allowed him to go underwater and recover these lost cargoes. Eads made a fortune from this work.*

After the war, the skilled, self-taught Eads built a triple-arch bridge over the Mississippi at St. Louis, pioneering many techniques in bridge building in the process. It was the largest bridge in the world at the time and the first to be built of steel. Later, Eads worked on freeing the Mississippi's channel of silt at New Orleans so the channel could handle shipping throughout the entire year.

This lithograph shows the bridge over the Mississippi that James Eads built in St. Louis, Missouri, after the Civil War.

Early in the war, the Confederates captured Norfolk Navy Yard, giving them access to the ship that became the ironclad *Virginia*. By the end of the war, the yard had changed hands again, but it had been reduced to little more than the rubble shown here.

unable to move. The *Virginia* fired on the ship repeatedly until it surrendered. A third Union ship, the *Minnesota*, also ran aground. As the day ended, the *Virginia* returned home, planning to finish off the *Minnesota* the next day. The damage done by the Confederate ship threw officials in the North into a panic.

A Historic Battle

When the *Virginia* appeared the next day, it was met by the Union's ironclad, the *Monitor*. Because the North had known that the South was working on the *Virginia*, it had rushed to build the *Monitor*. A funny looking vessel, the *Monitor* was simply a low hull with a central round turret that held two guns. Its design was revolutionary because the turret could turn, pointing the guns anywhere the captain wanted.

The *Monitor* and the *Virginia* fought an inconclusive battle. Neither ship could

"Likely the first move of the [Virginia] would be to come up the Potomac [River] and disperse Congress, destroy the Capitol and public buildings; or she might go to New York and Boston and destroy those cities."

Gideon Welles, describing the fears of Secretary of War Edwin Stanton on March 8, 1862

The *Monitor* (left) was dismissed as a tin can on a shingle by some, but it stood up to the pounding delivered by the *Virginia*.

break the armor of the other. The *Virginia* returned to Norfolk, never to damage the Union fleet again, while the *Monitor* stayed in the area, keeping the *Virginia* bottled up. In early May, Union land forces closed in on the navy yard, and the Confederates had to destroy the *Virginia* to prevent its capture.

Though the fight between the *Monitor* and the *Virginia* was a draw, it remains a historic battle (often known as the battle between the *Monitor* and the *Merrimac*). Steam had recently replaced sails for warships, and this battle showed that iron was replacing wood. A *London Times* reporter commented in 1862 that the British navy no longer had 149 first-rate ships but only two—Britain's two experimental ironclads. It was madness, the reporter said, to use any other kind of ship.

Other Ironclads

Both sides built other ironclads. The Union churned out several, many of which followed the *Monitor*'s design. The South's were built like the *Virginia*. One, the *Arkansas*, fought well at Vicksburg in 1863 but was destroyed by its crew to prevent its capture. The *Albemarle* caused considerable damage to Union ships off North Carolina until it was finally sunk by a mine. The *Tennessee* fought

The Union ship *Sassacus* rams the Confederacy's *Albemarle* (right) late in the war off North Carolina. Ironclads were tough boats; this action did not sink the *Albemarle*.

the Union fleet at Mobile Bay. Its story will be told in Chapter 7.

The *Hunley*

Ironclads were not the only naval innovations in the Civil War; there were also new designs for mines, or containers filled with explosives that blew up on contact. The Confederates turned anything they could find into a mine, including empty beer barrels.

The most remarkable advance, though, was the *H. L. Hunley*. This Confederate-built ship was a submarine. To power the ship, its seven crew members manually turned cranks that spun a propeller to push the ship

"She was a beautifully modeled boat, and worked to perfection."

James McClintock, chief designer of the *H. L. Hunley*

through the water. The interior was cramped; sailors had to sit hunched over. The *Hunley* rode just under the water's surface, with tubes reaching up to bring air inside. It had a difficult history, sinking in several trial voyages and killing several crew members as well as H. L. Hunley, who had helped finance the ship. After his drowning, the ship was named for him.

Despite its problems, the *Hunley* was used in combat once, earning it a place in history. On February 17, 1864, the ship stole into Charleston Harbor. It moved quietly underwater for 4 miles (6 km), to the *Housatonic*. The *Hunley* carried a bomb with 135 pounds (60

Ironclad warships were widely used for the first time in the Civil War. Relatively small, they were used for river fighting and coastal action and did not enter deep-sea waters.

kg) of gunpowder on the end of a pole. Sticking the bomb into the side of the *Housatonic*, the *Hunley* then backed off, detonating the bomb, which blasted a hole in the enemy ship and sunk it.

For the first time in history, a submarine had sunk a ship. The submarine's crew did not make it back to shore, however; the *Hunley* sank on the return trip.

The revolutionary *Hunley* sits on a Charleston dock awaiting its fateful, and historic, mission.

RECOVERING HISTORY

Undersea explorers have located two of the Civil War's most famous ships and even recovered all or part of them. In the 1970s, the Monitor was found where it had sunk off North Carolina late in 1862. Divers pulled up the engine, the propeller, and other ship parts. In 2002, crews hauled the entire gun turret out of the water. Inside lay the skeletons of two crew members plus many objects.

The H. L. Hunley was found in 1995. Five years later, the submarine was pulled from the sea. Scientists worked carefully to clean the silt out of the ship's interior, recovering the remains of the entire crew along with several objects.

Privateers and Raiders

~

The Confederates built two fast, powerful ships whose task was to sink the North's merchant ships. One of these raiders, the *Florida*, is shown here.

Failure of Privateers

While the blockade-runners tried to get needed goods into the South, the Confederates also had another trade-related mission—stopping Northern ships that carried goods. Since they lacked ships of their own at first, the Confederates tried recruiting ships as privateers. This effort was short lived, however. Britain and several other European nations had signed a treaty in 1856 that outlawed privateers. On June 1, 1861, Britain declared that privateers could not sell seized cargoes or ships in British ports. When other nations followed suit, recruiting privateers effectively ended because only the South remained as a reliable market for seized ships and their cargoes.

The Raiders' Goals

The Confederates' next weapon against Northern merchant ships was the commerce raiders, which were ships belonging to the Confederate navy. Like the privateers, they focused on attacking Northern merchant ships, not warships, hoping to disrupt the delivery of supplies to the North.

The South's first commerce raider was the *Sumter*. Commander Raphael Semmes had workers in New Orleans turn the one-time passenger steamer into a warship. Though Union ships were blockading that port, Semmes escaped out to sea in June of 1861. Over the next six months, he captured seventeen ships. Semmes steamed around the Atlantic Ocean, cleverly eluding capture and using legal arguments to convince officials in **neutral** ports to give him needed coal and other supplies. By the summer of 1862, though, Union ships had trapped the *Sumter* in Gibraltar on the southern coast of Spain. Semmes sold the vessel and took his officers to their next assignment, the *Alabama*.

The Confederate hero of the effort to build commerce raiders was Commander James D. Bulloch. A former U.S. Navy officer, Bulloch had energy, intelligence, and diplomatic skill. He reached Britain in June 1861 and quickly made deals with two British companies to build two

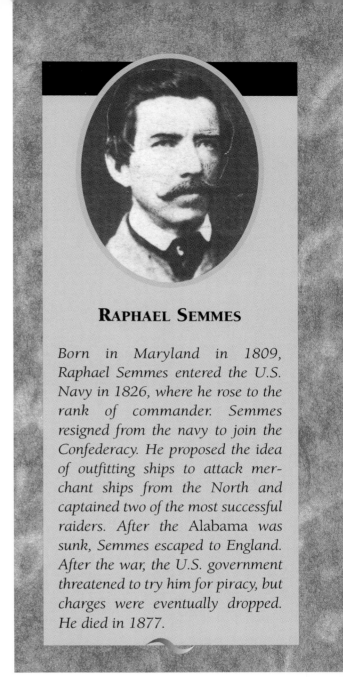

RAPHAEL SEMMES

Born in Maryland in 1809, Raphael Semmes entered the U.S. Navy in 1826, where he rose to the rank of commander. Semmes resigned from the navy to join the Confederacy. He proposed the idea of outfitting ships to attack merchant ships from the North and captained two of the most successful raiders. After the Alabama was sunk, Semmes escaped to England. After the war, the U.S. government threatened to try him for piracy, but charges were eventually dropped. He died in 1877.

steamships. Bulloch managed to avoid breaking British law by having the ships built without military equipment, which was to be added later, after they had left Britain. Once they entered the Confederate navy, the ships were given the names *Florida* and *Alabama*.

Fire from the Union ship *Kearsarge* shattered the middle mast of the *Alabama* (right). Soon after, the Confederate ship sank.

Raiding Successes

From early 1863 to late 1864, the *Florida* destroyed several ships, some of them off New York. A Union ship captured the *Florida* in a Brazilian harbor, violating the neutrality of Brazil, which protested. Union commander Napoleon Collins, who had taken the *Florida*, was found guilty of breaking international law in a Union court-martial. Secretary of the Navy Welles showed that he was unwilling to punish Collins, however, and threw out the court's decision.

The *Alabama* was a far more successful raider. In two years of cruising the oceans, Semmes captured or destroyed more than sixty ships, including one warship. In June 1864, though, the *Alabama* met its end. The ship was in Cherbourg, France, for repairs. A Union ship, Captain John Winslow's *Kearsarge*, appeared offshore. Semmes steamed

"Semmes, of whom we have been so proud—he is a fool after all—risked the Alabama *in a sort of duel of ships! He has lowered the flag of the famous* Alabama *to the* Kearsarge. *Forgive who may! I cannot."*

Mary Boykin Chesnut, Southern diarist, 1864

his ship into the open water to fight. The action lasted only about an hour, and it ended disastrously for the Confederacy. The *Alabama* was badly damaged, and it sank.

Delicate Diplomacy

Meanwhile, Bulloch continued his efforts to build ships for the South. That task was difficult because Union diplomats tried to convince European governments that building the ships broke their declarations of neutrality. Indeed, Bulloch had been forced to sneak the *Alabama* out of Britain because the British government was about to ban its departure. After that, the British government paid even closer attention to his actions.

Still, Bulloch kept up his work, and in 1863, he commissioned the Laird shipyards in Liverpool, England, to build two ironclad ships equipped with rams. The "Laird rams" became the focus of a diplomatic crisis between the United States and Great Britain.

As the ships were being built, Bulloch became convinced that the British would not let him take them out of Britain and developed an elaborate plan to get around the neutrality laws. He arranged for a French company to buy them, supposedly for Egypt. Then, once they were out of Britain, he would buy the ships back. The U.S.

ambassador to Britain exposed the plan to the British government and protested sharply that letting the ships go would violate British neutrality. The British government, meanwhile, had grown increasingly embarrassed by the situation and, in September, ordered that the ships could not leave. Eventually, the British navy bought both ships.

Bulloch did not give up; he signed deals to build four more ships in France. Once again, U.S. diplomats protested. In 1864, the French government ordered that the ships had to be sold to some other country. Bulloch managed

THE TRENT AFFAIR

The Laird rams issue was not the first diplomatic dispute between the United States and Great Britain during the Civil War. Captain Charles Wilkes, a Union naval officer, caused a crisis back in 1861 when he seized two Confederate diplomats, James Mason and John Slidell, from the Trent, a British ship. The British were outraged at a clear violation of international law. They demanded an apology and the diplomats' release. The crisis ended when the United States said that Wilkes had acted without orders, and the diplomats were freed.

Officers and crew members of merchant ships captured by raiders were sometimes held in the Confederate raider ship's hold, as these captives of the *Alabama* were.

to obtain and arm one of the ships, but it did not reach U.S. waters until May 1865. The war, by then, was over.

Other Raiders

Of the other Confederate raiders besides the *Florida* and the *Alabama*, the most successful was the *Georgia*, but that raider had captured only eight ships when its career ended. Before the *Florida's* capture, one of its junior officers took a captured Union warship on a raiding expedition. It succeeded in destroying some ships, including a few harmless fishing vessels, before its crew was captured.

In the end, the raiders failed in their goal. While many ships were sunk, commerce between the North and Europe continued to flow. Northern merchants simply put their goods on ships flying the flags of neutral countries. Some of those ships were, in fact, American ships that had simply been transferred to foreign owners. Because they flew flags of neutral nations, Confederate ships could not seize them.

Daily Life on the Ships

CHAPTER SIX

Recruiting Crews

Throughout the war, both North and South had problems getting enough people to serve on ships' crews. The problem was especially difficult in the South, which did not have a strong **maritime** tradition. Secretary Mallory complained that many soldiers wanted to transfer to the navy but were stopped by their commanding officers who did not want to lose their troops. He convinced the Confederate Congress to pass a law against such blocking, but it made little real difference. Both sides tried various methods to fill their ships. Sometimes, they simply forced soldiers to become sailors to avoid the unpopular **draft** system.

Two sections of the navy had less difficulty getting recruits. As mentioned earlier, blockade-runners were often owned by foreign investors, and the crews on these

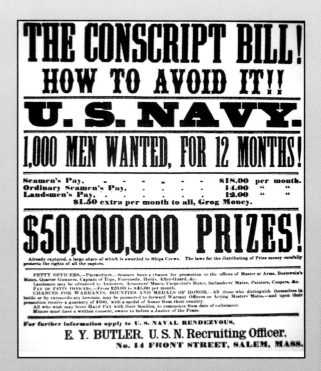

This Union poster tried to encourage Northerners to join the navy instead of being subject to the draft—the "conscript bill." The $50 million in prizes refers to the chance sailors had to share in the rewards of captured ships.

ships were often recruited in foreign lands, particularly Britain. The commerce raiders like the *Alabama* and the *Florida* also found it easier to find crews since sailors on these ships were paid in gold.

New recruits were first assigned to "receiving ships." There, they received uniforms and some basic training in navy life. Occasionally, the officers commanding these ships received requests for a number of sailors. They rounded up that number, who were then sent to active duty on a ship. The training time was often as short as a few days and rarely more than a few weeks.

Robert Smalls not only escaped himself, he also took along his wife, his children, his brother, and his brother's family.

African-American Sailors

Some crew members for both sides were African Americans. The South allowed free blacks to serve on shipboard. Not surprisingly, far more served for the North.

While the Union army was not convinced early in the war that having African-American soldiers was a good idea, the navy accepted blacks from the start. By 1865, 29,000 blacks had served in the navy. Most of these sailors did not have combat duty, but some did. Others played different vital roles. Several Southern blacks who knew the channels in coastal waters and rivers served as pilots on blockading ships. One was Robert Smalls, who joined the Union Navy by stealing a Southern ship and taking it out to the Union fleet blockading Charleston.

Daily Life

The sailors' days began early, at about five in the morning. The first few hours were spent cleaning the ship. This was particularly needed on steam-powered ships, as the soot from burning coal covered everything. Indeed, loading coal onto the ship typically left deposits of coal dust everywhere.

A group of African Americans aboard the USS *Vermont*. Most African-American sailors worked as seamen, firemen, and coal carriers.

Breakfast came at eight, but the food was meager. Sailors received little more than hard bread, salted meat, and coffee. Inspections followed the meal. On warships, officers paid special attention to the guns and to the metal tracks along which the guns moved. These had to be kept clean to make sure that they would work properly in combat. If the officers found problems, the rest of the morning was spent cleaning some more.

"While at the wheel of the Planter *as Pilot in the Rebel service, it occurred to me that I could not only secure my own freedom but that of numbers of my comrades . . . and, moreover, I thought that the* Planter *might be of some service to 'Uncle Abe.'"*

Robert Smalls, describing his escape in the *Planter*, 1864

Lunch was served at noon and included meat and vegetables along with coffee. Ships on blockade duty or shore patrols had an advantage over ships out to sea; they could buy fresh food from local farmers in season. Crews on blockade-runners or commerce raiders sometimes enjoyed treats they had taken from captured ships.

Afternoons were spent in training. Officers tried to vary each day's activities to cut down on the boredom that sailors suffered, but they could not eliminate it completely. Especially for sailors on blockade duty, the daily routine quickly became familiar and seemed to never end.

A small meal was served at 4:00. At 5:30, officers carried out another inspection. After that, sailors who were not on duty were free to do whatever they wanted. Many stayed above the deck as long as possible. Engine oil, burning coal, sweaty bodies, and damp wood made the mix of smells below decks unpleasant, and the lack of fresh air made it worse. Sailors slept below deck in hammocks that were crowded together. There was little comfort on board the ships.

THE "POWDER MONKEYS"

Some of those on board warships were young boys around twelve years old. These "powder monkeys" had a dangerous job during battle; they had to go into the ship's hold to pick up gunpowder packets that they carried to each gun crew.

Young boys were preferred for this work because they could move quickly and walk easily in the holds, which did not have much headroom. When the ship was not fighting, the powder monkeys served food to the officers and helped clean the ship.

A photographer caught a powder monkey in a rare moment of rest.

The *Monitor*'s crew relaxes on the ironclad's deck.

During the night, groups of offi-cers and sailors on four-hour shifts, called watches, looked after the ship. They made sure that it stayed on course, took messages from other ships in the fleet, and kept lookout for enemy ships. Crews on blockading ships kept a careful eye out for blockade-runners looking to escape during the night. If one was spotted, the crew was alerted and sprang to action.

"The life of a sailor is not one of a real and regular work. His hours of rest may not be uniform but they are more or less regulated. . . . [The] outlines [of tasks] are the same day after day."

Charles K. Mervine, Union sailor

CHAPTER SEVEN

Tightening the Noose

*"Damn the torpedoes! Full
speed ahead!"*

Admiral David Glasgow Farragut, at Mobile Bay, 1864

~

Seesaw in Texas

Both Union and Confederate navies were involved in fighting in Texas. The main goals there were the port cities of Galveston and Brownsville. These cities were captured by the Union in 1862 and 1863 but retaken by the Confederates. Union gunboats also tried to destroy the Confederacy's Fort Griffin on the Sabine River. Their failure to do so stopped a proposed invasion of Texas and left the South in control of that state.

Union Victory at Mobile Bay

By early 1864, Mobile, Alabama, remained the last major Gulf port east of Texas that blockade-runners could still use. That summer, the Union moved against it. In command was David Glasgow Farragut, who had been made a rear admiral after his victory at New Orleans.

Farragut had fourteen wooden ships and four **monitors**. He faced three Confederate forts and many mines, which were called torpedoes at the time, placed along the channel to force his ships closer to the fort's guns. The South also had a powerful ironclad, the *Tennessee*, in the bay, but only three gunboats to support it. Commanding the Southern fleet from the *Tennessee* was an old navy friend of Farragut's, Admiral Franklin Buchanan.

In the lower left, the ironclad *Tennessee* leads the small Confederate fleet out to meet the Union ships, led by the *Hartford*, as they steam past one of the two forts guarding the entrance to Mobile Bay in 1864.

On August 5, 1864, Farragut's fleet steamed into the bay. A leading ship, the monitor *Tecumseh*, struck a mine and quickly sank. Despite the dangerous mines, Farragut took the lead in the *Hartford*.

Union ships quickly disposed of two gunboats; the third, disabled, pulled away. The *Tennessee* put up a fierce fight, ramming two Union ships and blasting away at the *Hartford*. Still, faulty charges prevented all of its shots from going off. Meanwhile, Union ships were battering the *Tennessee*, blowing its smokestack in half and wounding many of the crew. After its rudder was destroyed, the ship could not steer. The *Tennessee* surrendered, ending the battle.

DAVID GLASGOW FARRAGUT

David Glasgow Farragut was one of the Union's naval heroes during the Civil War. Born in 1801 in Tennessee, he joined the Navy so young that he saw action in the War of 1812.

In late 1861, Farragut was given the assignment of capturing New Orleans. It was his idea to run his ships past the forts to take the city. He carried out the strategy brilliantly and easily took this important port early in 1862. The next year, Farragut's ships helped General Ulysses S. Grant capture Vicksburg, Mississippi. When Port Hudson, Louisiana, fell shortly thereafter, the North had complete control of the Mississippi River. Farragut's last success was the capture of Mobile Bay in 1864.

He became a full admiral in 1866, the first U.S. officer to reach that rank. He remained in the Navy until his death in 1870.

The ironclad *Tennessee* (right) pounds the *Hartford* under the eyes of Admiral Farragut, who is standing in his ship's rigging to see above the battle's smoke. (An officer tied a rope around the admiral so he would not fall off.)

THE SURRENDER OF THE *SELMA*

One of the Confederate gunboats at Mobile Bay was the Selma, commanded by Lieutenant Peter Umstead Murphey. Heavy fire from the Metacomet, under Commander James E. Jouett, forced the Selma to surrender. Murphey came on board Metacomet to surrender his sword, saying, "Captain Jouett, the fortunes of war compel me to tender you my sword." Jouett greeted his old friend Murphey with less formality: "Pat [Murphey's nickname], don't make a damned fool of yourself. I have had a bottle on ice for you for the last half hour."

Taking Charleston

With Mobile Bay gone, blockade-runners could only use the ports of the Carolinas, Charleston, and Wilmington. They became the next Union targets.

Charleston, South Carolina, had long been a thorn in the Union's side. Its strong defenses included two forts at the mouth of the harbor and several more inside. A major expedition, including a large Union fleet, had been mounted in 1863 to try to capture the city. However, Secretary Welles was not hopeful of the outcome. "As a general thing, such

Confederates lower mines into the water of Charleston harbor to make the channel too dangerous for Union ships to enter.

immense expeditions are failures," he wrote in his diary. Welles was right. After heavy fighting, the Union commander called off the attack.

The city remained firmly in Confederate control all through 1864, though blockading ships lurked offshore. During this standoff, the *Hunley* sank the *Housatonic*.

When Union general William T. Sherman's army marched from Savannah, Georgia, to North Carolina, however, it cut Charleston off from communication with any Southern forces inland. On February 18, 1865, the Confederates aban-

> *"I said to myself, 'here is a soldier who understands his profession and we have been fooling around with a problem that we didn't know what to do with.'"*
>
> Navy officer Stephen Luce in 1899, recalling his reaction to Sherman's plan for taking Charleston

doned Charleston without a fight. That same day, four blockade-runners entered the city, unaware of

This small Confederate force tried to hold Fort Fisher, but accurate fire from the ships off-shore (right) and overwhelming numbers helped the Union take the fort.

its fate. They were captured, and the Southern armies lost another chance to get valuable supplies.

The Falls of Fort Fisher and Wilmington

While the Union moved against Charleston, it also made plans to take Wilmington, North Carolina,

the other remaining Southern port. First, however, the North had to capture nearby Fort Fisher, which protected any blockade-runners that ran to and from Wilmington. In January 1865, a combined naval and land attack suffered heavy casualties but took Fort Fisher.

Wilmington became the lone source of the supplies that the

Confederate armies desperately needed. With Fort Fisher gone, the Union navy owning the seas, and Sherman's army advancing north, Wilmington's days were numbered, however. In late February, the South pulled its troops out of the city. Sherman's army entered the next day.

With no chance of being supplied, the Southern armies could not survive much longer. By early April, General Robert E. Lee knew he could no longer fight and surrendered his Army of Northern Virginia. Later in the month, Joseph E. Johnston surrendered the force that opposed Sherman. The war, in effect, was over.

"The red glare from the . . . burning vessels shone far and wide over the drifting ice of those savage seas. . . . When, one by one, the burning hulks went hissing and gurgling down into the treacherous bosom of the ocean, the last act in the bloody drama of the American Civil War had been played."

Anonymous eyewitness to the destruction of the whaling fleet by the *Shenandoah*, 1886

and the remainder held to transport the crews of the destroyed ships. All of this destruction occurred in June 1865, well after the Confederate armies surrendered in May. Finally, in August 1865, the ship's captain learned that the war had ended, and he returned with the ship to Great Britain.

The Last Battles at Sea

Late in the war, the Confederates thought they saw one remaining target in the North's merchant fleet—whaling ships. The *Shenandoah* reached the whaling fleet in the Pacific Ocean. In just one week, it captured twenty-four of the fleet's fifty-eight ships. Twenty were burned,

THE *ALABAMA* CLAIMS

The war's end did not end all the issues that the naval conflicts had created. The U.S. government demanded that the British repay it for the shipping destroyed by Confederate vessels built in Britain. The cases were called "the Alabama claims," but they involved the actions of other ships as well. The issue threatened to damage American and British relations. A special commission ruled that Britain owed $15.5 million to the United States for the damage caused by the Florida, *the* Shenandoah, *and the* Alabama. *Nearly $2 million more was awarded as damages in other cases. The British government promptly paid the claims.*

1861 *Apr. 12:* Confederates fire on Fort Sumter, South Carolina, marking the beginning of the Civil War.
Apr. 17: South offers to commission privateers, hoping to destroy Union merchant shipping.
Apr. 19: Union proclaims blockade of Southern ports to prevent Confederacy from receiving supplies.
June 30: CSS *Sumter* escapes blockade at New Orleans and begins attacking Northern merchant ships.
Aug. 27–28: Union forces capture forts on Hatteras Inlet, North Carolina, blocking Confederacy's access to ports.
Nov. 7: Union forces seize Port Royal, South Carolina, key point on coast.
Nov. 8: Captain Charles Wilkes seizes diplomats James Mason and John Slidell, launching diplomatic crisis between Union and Great Britain.
Dec. 26: Union agrees to release Mason and Slidell.

1862 *Feb. 6:* Union captures Fort Henry on Tennessee River.
Feb. 16: Union captures Fort Donelson on Cumberland River, gaining control of western Tennessee.
Mar. 8: CSS *Virginia* sinks two ships off Norfolk, Virginia, in first combat involving an ironclad ship.
Mar. 9: CSS *Virginia* and USS *Monitor* fight off Norfolk in first battle in history between two ironclads.
Apr. 8: Union captures Island No. 10 on Mississippi River, giving it control of upper Mississippi.
Apr. 24: David Farragut runs his fleet past the forts below New Orleans, opening the city to Union capture.
Aug. 17: *Florida* is commissioned in Confederate navy.

Aug. 24: *Alabama* is commissioned in Confederate navy.
Dec. 31: USS *Monitor* sinks off Cape Hatteras, North Carolina.

1863 *Apr. 6:* Union attack on forts in Charleston Harbor fails, allowing it to remain in Confederate hands.
July 3: Confederates at Vicksburg surrender, giving up last major stronghold on Mississippi.
July 8: Confederates at Port Hudson, Louisiana, surrender, completing Union control of Mississippi River.
Sep. 5: British prohibit the Laird rams from leaving Britain, preventing South from gaining powerful new ships.

1864 *Feb. 17:* CSS *Hunley* sinks the USS *Housatonic*, the first time a submarine sinks a ship.
June 19: USS *Kearsarge* sinks CSS *Alabama* off Cherbourg, France.
Aug. 5: Farragut captures Mobile Bay, giving Union control of Gulf coast.
Oct. 7: USS *Wachusett* captures CSS *Florida* at Bahia, Brazil, ending the career of another Confederate raider.

1865 *Jan. 15:* Union forces capture Fort Fisher, North Carolina, one of last remaining ports in Confederate hands.
Feb. 18: Confederates evacuate Charleston, South Carolina, losing another source of supply by sea.
Feb. 22: Union forces take Wilmington, North Carolina, removing the last source of supplies for the Confederacy.
May 26: Last major Confederate army surrenders.
June: CSS *Shenandoah* captures almost half of Union whaling fleet, not realizing war has ended.

blockade: to prevent enemy ships from carrying goods into or out of ports during a war.

blockade-runners: cargo vessels that can penetrate a blockade or evade enemy ships stationed in a port. "Running a blockade" means to slip past the ships guarding a port.

Border States: the states on the northern edge of the southern states, where there was slavery, but it was not as strong a part of society as in the deeper South; includes Delaware, Maryland, Kentucky, and Missouri, all of which remained with the Union.

cabinet: a group of advisers chosen by the head of a nation.

commission: the authority to act for a specific purpose.

Confederacy: also called "the South;" another name for the Confederate States of America, the nation formed by the states that had seceded—Virginia, Tennessee, North Carolina, South Carolina, Georgia, Alabama, Mississippi, Louisiana, Texas, Arkansas, and Florida.

diving bell: a large, submergible vessel supplied with air for underwater work.

draft: a law that requires men of a certain age to join the military.

garrison: the body of troops defending a fort.

inaugural: relating to an inauguration, a formal ceremony in which an individual is installed into political office.

maritime: relating to the sea, shipping, navigating, or sailors.

merchant fleet: vessels that carry goods for trade.

monitor: an ironclad with a low, flat deck and one or more gun turrets.

neutral: not taking any side in a fight.

rams: projections on a ship's prow, or front, used to batter against another ship.

reinforcements: soldiers added to a force to make it stronger.

secede: to formally withdraw from an organization; in the case of the Civil War, it means to leave the United States.

Union: also called "the North;" another name for the United States of America, which, after secession, included Maine, New Hampshire, Vermont, Massachusetts, Rhode Island, Connecticut, New York, New Jersey, Pennsylvania, Delaware, Maryland, Ohio, Michigan, Indiana, Illinois, Kentucky, Wisconsin, Minnesota, Iowa, Kansas, Missouri, Oregon, and

California; in 1863, West Virginia seceded from Virginia and entered the Union as a separate state.

Further Resources

These books and web sites cover the naval battles during the Civil War and the people leading and fighting those battles:

WEB SITES

www.civilwaralbum.com The Civil War Album has modern and wartime photos of Civil War sites and maps.

www.civilwarhome.com Includes links to a number of articles on the naval war, with an introduction and articles on types of ships, sailors' lives, and the organization of both navies.

www.civil-war.net The Civil War Home Page Web site includes selected documents by Lincoln and others, including entries of soldiers' diaries and letters home, a detailed time line, and images of war.

www.homepages.dsu.edu/jankej/ civilwar/ civilwar.htm An index web site lists numerous articles on a wide range of Civil War topics, including the navies.

sunsite.utk.edu/civil-war/warweb.html The American Civil War web site contains a number of links to resources, including images of wartime, biographical information, and much more.

BOOKS:

Adelson, Bruce. *David Farragut: Union Admiral.* Philadelphia, PA: Chelsea House, 2002.

Bolotin, Norman. *The Civil War A to Z: A Young Readers' Guide to over 100 People, Places, and Points of Importance.* New York: Dutton Books, 2002.

Campbell, R. Thomas. *Gray Thunder: Exploits of the Confederate States Navy.* Shippensburg, PA: Burd Street Press, 2002.

Clinton, Catherine. *Scholastic Encyclopedia of the Civil War.* New York: Scholastic Books, 1999.

Harlowe, Jerry L. *Monitors: The Men, Machines, and Mystique.* Gettysburg, PA.: Thomas Publications, 2001.

Hicks, Brian, and Schuyler Kropf. *Raising the* Hunley: *The Remarkable History and Recovery of the Lost Confederate Submarine.* New York: Ballantine Books, 2002.

Kirchberger, Joe. *The Civil War and Reconstruction: An Eyewitness History.* New York: Facts On File, 1991.

O'Brien, Patrick. *Duel of the Ironclads: The* Monitor *vs. the* Virginia. New York: Walker and Co., 2003.

Stern, Philip Van Doren. *The Confederate Navy: A Pictorial History.* New York: Da Capo Press, 1992.

Index

Page numbers in *italics* indicate maps and diagrams.